Hi Abi.

# Sui

Michael Indemaio

Acrylic Verbs Press
New York, New York

Acrylic Verbs Press
New York, NY


ISBN: 0-9713503-5-3

Library of Congress Control Number: 2003097941


Cover Art by Keri Lynn Kroboth

Manufactured in the United States of America

# Contents

# Preface

Knowledge is power and power corrupts. To be corrupt is to be normal, and to be normal is to be safe. It was my intention for this book to be anything but safe. It was my intention for these poems to know nothing. Under the maybe flawed assumption that anything could remain unsaid, I have found myself as myself, writing this preface, although I myself know nothing.

When these living poems wrote themselves, they were one at a time introduced to me, as miniscule evidences of the powerful Yes of every Is. They were made and making. They were alive. If they said anything it was always an affirmation of an existence so real it remains always undefined. These poems sang to me dreamlike about individuality and truth.

It is my belief that when measuring with anything from the molecule to the Milky Way, there is always the triumphantly immeasurable individual. There is always the astoundingly true self. Suddenly there are poems and questions. Suddenly there are snowflakes and the laughter of children—and life, maybe choking or embracing, but everything always happening. Suddenly we are not merely here, we are alive. All this becomes possible only with that perfectly unique and beautifully flawed actual individual, that any every primary unit of unmeasurement—me, you, us, ourselves. It is my possibly flawed belief that anyone who thinks otherwise has probably been forced to know something.

I can only imagine that these poems will eventually meet such a person. One of the supposed people who know many things, and who think you should be educated, and who by educated probably mean indoctrinated. One of those who have acquired a considerable amount of that flimsy concept called power, via some soi-distant society in which it is a prize and in which everyone knows and everyone is normal and safe and medicated and in which sameness trumps uniqueness, and beauty is dead. It is my fully foolish hope that if these poems were to meet such a person, they would not speak. I would like to think that they would not know enough to argue. Instead it is my childlike desire that these poems speak only to those who know nothing, and feel everything. That they speak only to any and every perfectly unique and beautifully flawed actual individual.

Michael Indemaio

# The Circumference of A Wound

*I was running from my savior and I never thought I'd waver I just*
*try to stumble on, then backwards downhill feet-a-tangled, head's*
*gone over heart's all mangled, spinning tripping slipping I'm*
*afraid to lose my grip and...* I believe we hit a wall.
I sing...
      I spin...
            I fall.

Regrets are wounds that terrify
So supplement and verify
This is the very last poem that I'll write for you.

You know, you do not have to love me
Just because I think you should.
You don't even have to call me
Just because you said you would,
And I don't have to walk a mile
Just to meet you in the rain
And I don't have to try or cry
Just because all you ever gave me
Was your sorrow, was your pain.
Just know that singing to your smile
I got stuck in the refrain.
Yes, I get stuck in my refrains.

And my word-dependent
Thought-regressing
Shadow-sucking love,
Swallows stars,
Puts hearts in jars,
And plays piano on the moon.
This is the unwording of a fool.

1

And there's nothing we can do.
Because you're still the most beautiful thing
That I've ever seen dirtied,
You're a remarkable angel
Among other reasons,
Because you can make me feel worried.
Because it's so damn easy to hurt me.
And if there is a God,
Then I think he needs to hurry.

To hurry up and kill me
Hurry up and spill me
Upon the carpet of your dreams,
Broken glass knows how to bleed,
Charging forward I recede,
Blind belief wounds,
As it impedes.

There are things—are you listening?
There are things, all around us
That are so constant we can't see them.
As a result we never miss them
Never notice that we need them.
The greatest way to go unnoticed
I've noticed,
Is to constantly be there.
Another rotting truth, that quite simply isn't fair.

And by this I don't mean
That I'm not there if you need me
But I cannot be a constant
I cannot allow you to lead me.

And I cannot live alone
In your peripheral love,
Although I'll love you forever
I know when too much is enough.

Because I gave you my words
But you wanted my soul,
So just stab me again
So I can see the pain go,
Just put a hole in my heart
So the hurt can depart,
This time I'll build my well being
From the end to the start.
Because I wanted your heart
But you gave me your tears
And in the end they've confirmed
All my pride's greatest fears.

So let me say this, one more time,
Thank you. Thank you for the pain.
Goodbye, I'm sorry, and I'll miss you,
But I get stuck in my refrains.
That's right, I get stuck in my refrains.

I sing…
      I spin…
            I fall.

## Devoid of a Miracle

Left behind and devoid of a miracle
Can you imagine how much I think of you?

My knees are weak but dependable
Like my inner thoughts.
When you're alone unless you're lonely
Your mind searches for what your heart demands,
Alternate sources of energy.
On moonlight nights
There are rivers raging everywhere.
Everything is liquid unless it is rage.
In this life anything can be everything
If it moves without remorse.
Someday miracles will emerge as flowers,
Petals in the rivers,
Which will be merely water
And my energies will be eternal.
Reincarnation will be nothing more
Than a new day. The morning sun.
It is hard to be left behind
When you can't stop moving.
I think of you when I need to link the processes
Drawing energy from distant motions
When my knees are too weak
To break through waterless rage
I use your energy
In the form of tomorrow's light
Or a petal in a river.
Knowing,
Somewhere beyond me
There must be a miracle.

# City Numbers

There are over 3 million people living
In Brooklyn today.
It is the largest part of the city
By population. Bigger than Houston.
The former home of the Dodgers,
It also has the most churches.
I live in Queens
The land of cemeteries, and diners.
It is the largest part of the city
By land.

It's been the rainiest spring and I guess
Beginning of summer
I or anyone, seems to remember here.
I hear Seattle is lovely, very rainy.
That's the home of grunge music
And chain coffeehouses.
It seems every Jeckyl has its Hyde.
With all this rain
It's hard to keep a healthy mind.

In a city of 8 million
I wonder what number I am.
I wander the storied streets
Taking longer paths
I know to be less busy.
I wonder what trick of fate
Allowed me to be born
In this hub of excitement and sin.
This randomly synchronized
Colossal creature, always
Moving, racing, offering

More free will than God
Probably imagined he created.

I stop in random places
For a seat and a glass of whatever
They're selling.
Paying mostly for the newness of the moment.
I wonder if it was ever intended
For my quiet contemplation
To be their currency.
I stop in familiar places
Alive with the comfort of memories.
I wonder if the memories are
Quietly in the background
Dictating the path of my travels.

I want to know why it is
That I wasn't born in Brooklyn
Or Seattle.
Is it all the cemeteries that lead me
To these sulking strolls?
Would more churches stop me
From doubting God's intentions
For this place?
Why won't it stop raining?
Why am I the one
Intent on strolling through it?
Was all of this predestined?
Was it all dictated
By the impossible to compute,
Limitless occurrences of my life?
Was I sent to Queens for a reason,

Or was it Queens that sent me here?

I walk over to the park
Where I once spun around
Until I was dizzy enough
And fell down,
Because it amused me.
I sit on a wet stone and
Watch the giant drops
Drop in their puddles,
Limitless and purposeful.
The ripples spread astoundingly,
And I think, perhaps,
It was me all along.
Never predestined, dictated, formed
Or controlled.
Perhaps always controlling
Diving headfirst with a splash
Creating ripples and enjoying the journey.

In a city of 8 million,
I am one.
The number is insignificant.

## Tomorrow is a Demon

If tomorrow is a demon
Then today's a dragon slayed
And if children are our future
Let adults be things passé.
If forever may seem daunting
Then let children leave their marks
And if eternity is darkness
Make every moment be a spark.
Because children are eternal
And eternal never ends
And there's not a speck of darkness
When Always lights Again.
Let the magic future bend.

## The Park

Sitting in the park, where we sat once before
Sitting in the dark, where I grew as a boy.
Someone once told me about embraces of joy
My fingers picked at the grass
Dug at the dirt
Someone once said it was too cold to be thinking.
The dirt of corruption, the fingers of fate.

Sitting in the park, where we sat once before
Someone walks in silence, someone walks a dog.
I've seen the sunglasses of sorrow
On the shoes of a child
And someone once told me I spend too much time
Like this.
I do spend time that's true.
Someone once said I could only blame me.
I know now that this park is self-evident,
I blame tulips, dig fingers, pick words.

Someone once said it was too cold to be thinking
Dark in the evening
We were floating on air. Elevated, windy
Blamed time, blamed myself.
I know the sting was goodnight,
I know the wind meant go home.
Someone once told me about embraces of joy
And we huddled for warmth.

The boy at the park
He blames tulips, thinks warmly
It's self-evident.
He buries fate in the dirt.

## He Takes Comfort in Her Sadness
## Or at Least Her Sincerity in Confronting It

As if it was somehow a bother and then
I thought maybe that's how you've been
How you've been and how you've been treated
And I'm sure you've seen more
          I have a notoriously short attention span
I must be missing something
But you look at me as if to apologize
For what I wonder?
          This is the most honest moment—
                    A moment only?

I am busy burying your eyes into memory.

Should I find your sadness tragic?
Because I mean I do of course,
But tragic only as much as amazing can be,
(Honest perfect person is alive)
          You'll have to excuse my loneliness.
It's been several breakdowns since I've met a person.

Either you've rehearsed this or there is no delay
Heart to mind to voice
                    To me, thank you
For sending me recklessly on forward knowing
I've been sent spinning you're beautiful, thank you.

It almost does feel rehearsed.
So comfortable, we must have practiced it.

## Prayer

Forever and ever and ever amen
Christ is my savior and God is my friend.
Tomorrow is hollow today is black matter
When the moments are cold, the daydreams will shatter,
It's hard to be pointless when you're splashing a grin
Labor is healthy but money is sin
Sin is corruption erupting your soul
And it's hard to be human if it's hard to be whole.

Alone I can stand as a unified piece
And pray to my friend while I'm down on my knees
Or spin like a lifetime, until I fall down
And know that the sky is the sea is the ground,
Up may be down if down may be up
I can drink from the sky, I can live in a cup
I can plan to be something that doesn't exist
And explain to the world that I know what it is.

If your voice doesn't echo then no one can hear you
And it's hard to be home if there's nobody near you
I will wholly keep moving and I'll keep asking how
Living alive like there's nothing but now,
I will never give up and I'll keep asking when
Forever and ever and ever amen.

## Letters

Dearest Nearest,
For the past 6 days, I've been searching for answers. For the past 6 years, I've been searching for answers. For the longest time, I had been searching for you. It's not that you've answered anything, beyond maybe my search, but you were the only thing I never had to question. I knew I would miss you, but I knew you had to go, and so I tried to hold off the first letter, as long as I could. I lasted 6 days. When I first fell in love with you, I knew only that I wanted to be in love with you.

Write back soon,
Far too far

Darling, repeat after me: "I do not know you. You are not the one who lights my days." When you fell in love with me, you did not want to be in love with me. You've always wanted nothing more than to have someone break your heart. In time you will realize that I couldn't even do that right. You and I are helpless. Not just with you and I, but in all ways.

Forget me,
Never Gone

Never Forgotten,
I am not a pet on the side of the road. You can not make my heart stop following. If you can't come back, then I will come to you. I am tired of being helpless. Your eyes have always been a little more honest than a sunrise. You are still what lights my days. You have been gone for 17 now. I can be gone, with you, tomorrow.

Always with love,
Tomorrow

12

Darling, I can't take any more. Your love is a love for letters. We have to deal in reality. Forget me, or this will destroy me. Do not write back.

Love always,<br>Yesterday

Hi… it's been a few months. How are you? I've been thinking of you. I hope you're settled. Forgive me if it's not what you want to hear, but I still miss you terribly. Nothing has really changed here. Please write back.

Always and regardless,<br>Unchanged

Hello dear. I'm sorry I didn't write back. I'm coming home next month. I hope I can see you. Everything is fine, and nothing is right. Candles refuse to dance, and the moonlight is cold. If you can remember me, forgive me. For the past 6 months, I have been searching for answers. I don't know if there are any. The sunsets here are all lies.

I hope we never write letters again.

## In my Head, In a Box

My boss chopped off my head one day
Kicked it around
And sent it air mail to my family.

The insurance doesn't cover any
Homicidal management
Or decapitation layoffs,
So the doctors tried their best.
They shocked my eyes with tiny paddles
And taped my screaming mouth
And they hooked me to computers
To try to stabilize my brain.
They called my boss for information
Asking if my body could still work,
He said my body's working fine
And was employee of the month.
The doctors said some wounds don't heal
But with treatment I'd get by
And they put my head inside a box
So that my kin could take me home.
They were told to keep me medicated
And to let me watch TV,
Twice a day,
When my body's out at work.
They said books would be too stressful
As would any kind of thought
And I could no longer see my body
Or attempt to reattach.
And so my boss has been promoted
And my body got a raise,
And I've been watching daytime TV
And I've been medicated well,

And while resting in my lonely box
With my memories and thoughts,
I wonder what the reason is
That they won't untape my mouth.

## Still

The newspapers have stars in their eyes
And the homeless have newspaper beds.

I've taken to giving them
Just enough money to shock them.
It's an irresponsible habit.
I know I can't really help
But goodness should be flaunted for amusement.
I guess I'm still looking for something.
For something beautiful alive and inspiring,
Something not at all still.

"Breaking News:
Someone famous is divorcing someone else famous
And being sued by someone not famous.
See page seventeen for details
About people starving somewhere
You may or may not have heard of."

That's a strange thing for someone to sleep on.

A young woman sits dirty and tired
By a coffee cup on the street.
Her sign says
"Must leave city
ASAP
I only need $25"
Her cup contains maybe
Two dollars in change
And a lighter.
She needs to get moving
But she's sitting terribly still.

That's a strange way for someone to be living.

"Someone famous revitalizes their career
With a blockbuster movie, knocking
Someone else famous down to two
At the box office.
Their pants will be on sale at next week's auctions.
Their lives will be on sale at a newsstand near you."

On the streets, people are losing hope.
Their lives are on sale daily.
For two dollars and a lighter
The bed is free.

Still, they must feel cheated.

## Cracking Morality

Console everyone's cracking morality
Because it doesn't matter.

Let he among us
Who throws a stone
Get glass within his eyes.

## Growing Pains

The plastic bag over my head drags me up the hall
And I am 12 years old again.
I have a lifetime to discover.
I will spend years, searching for the child.

The umbrella swings at my jumping legs
And I tumble down the stairs.
Through my one open eye, I cry
At the hungry faces in the crowd
Knowing somehow
About being thrown out bus doors
Stomped down on the street
Threatened on rooftops
And being knocked off my feet.
My throat being lifted high to the wall,
And the taste, of blood and dirt.
Learn it early,
The future awaits without mercy.

There will be years for isolation
And disastrous self-denial.
I will find a cynicism
More dangerous than switchblades,
And an apathy
Both violent and cruel.
There will be unexplained tears of frustration.
They will be so bitter
It will leave me longing for the taste,
Of blood and dirt.

I will hang on with weary arms
Until I finally learn to let go.

I will swallow memories like sleeping pills
Shutting any light that reveals a shadow.

I will learn how to love, how to forget
How to survive, and how to run.
I will learn how to make survival a reflex
Not an option.
As I try to find myself, I will revive a lost child.
I will stroll into my life—quiet and proud.

I laugh recklessly, and sleep in the grass,
My thick vulnerable skin rests without remorse
And I awake to take my place,
Parting the air as I walk,
Displacing whatever intrudes.
I embark upon the tasks of the moment
And see faces circle and stare.
The eyes narrow peering through me
And the voices nick at my skin.
I am discovered, threatened and panicked.
My heart pounds and it becomes hard to breathe.
I can feel the bag tighten again
And I am being dragged down the hall.
I am 12 years old and afraid.
I am a child, I am that child,
That child is me.
I remember.

I struggle quiet and proud
Ripping the bag off my head
And tossing it in defiance,
A gesture to say quietly

That they have chosen the wrong child,
That I have been here before.
I jump to my feet and take off running—
But not in the direction I came from.
The idea is to never go backwards,
The idea is to never go back.
Carrying on with my life
Quiet and proud.

## Jewelry Box

Take that ring off the finger it won't fit on,
Know you weren't worth the roses that you spit on.

I can't waste my soul with hatred
To disguise my soulful failures
While my mental isolation
Has been custom-made and tailored.
I can't stand here and demand here
That you try to understand dear—
Take the thorns out of your fingers
Take the rings out from your eyes,
Take my heart and call it sickly
Take my faith and call it lies.

If it takes you to be angry,
If you really have to hate me,
Before you know you have to leave,
Then take the gems and broken stems
And take the heart off of my sleeve.
There is no us left to retrieve.

If you somehow now don't hate me
And you still think you can save me,
If I'm still the one you wish on
And it's anger you insist on,
Know you weren't worth the roses that you spit on.

## Live Fiction

I live fiction and write poetry,
It's part of my instant gratification addiction.
I can't help it, growing up in the 80's
In a push-button, quick-fix, fast-high society
Microwaves and cocaine
                    God Bless America
I live fiction and breathe propaganda,
I can't help it, growing up in my mind
Open and flowing
More intent on taking in than giving out
Shiny birthday boxes
Lotteries and lattes
A dollar here a dollar there
$9.99, a penny for your thoughts
Take one, leave one
                    Open and flowing
Taxes and surcharges may apply
I can't help it, I have an overactive imagination
Nobody told me it was meant to be lethargic
(Power nap dreams during rocking chair seasons)
I can't help it, I'm a product of my surroundings
Surrounded and self-centered
            I live fiction and die in reality
And when given a choice,

I choose life.

## Doing the Math

| | |
|---|---|
| I add myself to your absence | $1 + 0 =$ |
| And find only myself | $1$ |
| I multiply by all I have | $1 \times 1 =$ |
| And I still have nothing else, | $1$ |
| I subtract it from the equation | $1 - 1 =$ |
| And find only your absence | $0$ |
| I try to divide the issues | $0 \div 1 =$ |
| And I find that nothing happens. | $0$ |

Our love has been splintered
From a whole into a fraction
We have made ourselves parts
Of the same abstraction,
Because I've been divided by your absence
And as a result I don't exist
There is no common denominator,
There is nothing for you to miss.

$1 \div 0 =$ (undefined)

## Taken from My Notebook,
## Dated but Untitled

It's all so clear from the depths of this confusion,
And somehow all she knows
Is that something is wrong with her.
What she beautifully tragically somehow amazingly misses
Is that <u>wrong</u> is one of those made up words,
And what she knows and calls this
From eight miles above her blood
Is everything magic about herself.

But nothing that magic powerful unique
(So impossible and perfect fiction
It could only be real, the only true real)
Could possibly be wrong, but right so right
That I would sit in that hot rain with her
Until my thinning self-made existence
Deteriorating with neglect
Completely melted into the private ground.
And I would laugh smile and sing my own death.
We all want to die for a good cause.

I like to pretend I know things, or at least live like I might,
And this is because I know certain important truths.
I know that so much is fake,
That if you want to be wise and correct
And a whole list of other virtues,
Then you must make your own reality—
Form your own worlds
                    —and set your own bounds.
She amazingly is one of those few
Who truly knows things
Independent of her own manifestations.

She, in her every molecule of being,
Somehow has a subtle and sublime understanding
Of the immaterial plain we all work on.
Everyday throwing illusions at each other hollow etc.

So what's to come?

What's to come of this solitary dream girl
Running through the rain
To find mortals who will make her weep
At her own angelic glory?
She will go on, on the wings of tears
Like the ones I broke
With toys called maturity intelligence and hate.

And perhaps I will have to watch when she learns to fly,
And then I will spend the rest of forever
Writing out the remaining always present impressions
She has left me with.
Also perhaps she will always be running
(Because I know she cannot stop to sit with me,
Forever in the rain,
Because I am not that magic)
And perhaps as she runs I will always follow,
And always be waiting around corners of destiny
Where she will always curiously find me
From time to time always her greatest ally.

There are so many possibilities,
Almost any of which sit fine with me
Though I know the sadness of writing her memory
For eternity

Would be a festering painful death—
But even that, the most beautiful imaginable.

Of course I have my favorites though,
The dreams I've invented—
Little loops of logic allowing me to see future realities
I only pray I can create on this mysterious plain.

My secret hope lies in the pain of her wings.
Because if this is truly a powerful hurt
Then it doesn't seem unreasonable to expect it for myself
(And indeed I have at times thought it likely that
I will eventually know every great pain available to me).

So my secret hope is that she will,
In her magic and unrecognized wisdom,
Fix my broken wings
So that I may follow closely as she flies,
Writing down her every gesture on rain soaked pages,
Crying laughing and singing
To the glorious magic angelic pain
She has so graciously in her confusion
Shared with sad make-believe me.

## 64 Crayons

64 crayons crying color color world...
Orange skies pink eyes blue grass—
A child who doesn't know what blue grass sounds like
And who has never had the misfortune
Of pink eye.

Young and creative, he lives in a primary color world.
His mother can never afford the 64 box.
It's not required,
But the lucky kids have it anyway.

"Can I use your crayon sharpener?"
"Sure"—so proud, so pitying.
It doesn't matter
Because at least he gets to use it.

"Hey can I borrow your gold and silver?"
"In a minute."

64 crayons crying color color world…
A red heart white word valentine card
Says "love you mom,"
And awaits its gold and silver trim.
The child is too young to know,
But he will one day learn,
How unimportant
The gold and silver is,
To the heart.

## In the Corner

Over here.
> In the corner over here.

Take your glass glare from my throat.
It is melting in the corner's desert
And my struggled breathing
Is blowing it into frightening shapes.
The sky is crumbling down on me
Raining dirt, a sirocco's howl
It gets hotter and hotter and
> There, distorted

I see you
> Laughing, splashing water

  Smiling and dancing
> Flower petals and fruit.

My distorted mirage, over here
I can hardly breathe, help
I pray to your eyes, I am weak.
> There, your hand

Large looming like the hand of God
It is coming, distorted still
It will scoop me up
To flower petals and fruit,
It is getting clearer
Then
> Earthquake.

I am tumbling and tossed
And the desert is destroyed.
When I awake
The sky is crumbling
And it is as it was.

Somewhere, you flip an hourglass
Unaware that I live inside
In the corner.

## Emotional Release #8

My bloodshot eyes hear cold dead words
And cynic pissings from those who know.
Leaking brains wrapped in cellophane.
I'm sick of how you know.
Proving dominance is still the pastime of the weak.
You think I don't see you?
You think I don't hear you?
Don't belittle my intelligence.
I've drank thorns for a buzz.
I've gone in and out like off and on.
Like a lightswitch in your dreams.
I've seen things that would turn your filth green.
Let me assure you, you do not know what I mean.
So don't lie to me, and then call me a friend.
Don't look at me. Don't challenge me.
Stop searching for my pride.
I see you, and I pity you.
Now please, excuse me while I digress—
I want to talk about begins, instead of ends.
About why the world resides,
In the skies of her eyes.
Because I'm tired, of how you know.
I'm tired of how you think.
I'm tired of how you hurt.
I'm tired of how you hate.
I'm tired of how you lie.
I'm tired…
       I'm tired…
             I'm… tired.

You know, I once saw a starving goddess
Give her mouth to an aspiring young lawyer.

Then, when they jumped through the looking glass,
They both just bled…

I've recently learned
That there are two kinds of silence.
It's always been my most amazing symptom.
See, I used to live, in the two breathless seconds
Between tracks 3 & 4
Of every album I've ever heard.
It was a stagnant, melancholy, motionless,
And frightening kind of silence.
But now,
The eyes of my eyes and the heart of my heart,
Have found that there is another
Better, kind of silence.
This silence smiles and sings
The songs of the evening before.
It is calm comfortable triumphant and dynamic.
It is the sound of a sleeping muse.
It is the trumpets of a magic begin.
It does not know, how to be insincere.

By this dear—I mean you're beautiful.
I mean only that you are an alchemist to my world,
And I love the way
You make moments which breathe.
Nows.
Not tomorrows, not yesterdays, not todays—
Just nows.
I can't take anymore destruction.
I can't take anymore people who know.
I want nothing scripted, and nothing destined.

I want ones instead of twos,
Wholes instead of parts,
And questions instead of answers.
Today, let's not worry about answers.
Today, let's jump in a painting,
Or soak in a song.
Let's fly somewhere,
Perhaps on the light beams from a perfect
Heartfelt smile.
Let's create nows,
In a million different ways.
There are no scripts, there are no answers,
There are no recipes or rules.

Anything is possible; everything is true.

Have you ever seen someone topple the sky
With a motion of their hand?
—Because I have.
Have you ever seen someone make the sun shine
With a flicker of their eyes?
Have you ever seen someone's shadow
Try to hug them while they were sad?
Have you ever seen someone make the tides rise
Simply by standing?
Have you ever seen someone make the world stop
With a simple whisper?

Well, have you ever seen yourself sneeze?
Have you ever seen what you look like
When you laugh so hard you turn red?
Have you ever seen

The happy curious startled shimmer
Of your eyes,
When they first see something
Excitingly and delightfully new?
Because I have.

Fairy-tale goddess,
Too good to be untrue,
Thank you for your moments,
Thank you for you.
Thank you for the ashes of your cigarette.
Thank you for you.

Just please, tell me a story.
I'm very tired.

## The Varied Tempo of A Heartbeat

The consistency of irregularity
Is soothing.
What's next is more of the same old newness.

When I'm talking you're listening
Teacher used to say,
   Teach her how to stay
   Why do dreams go away?

Dreams aren't real
They're only for nighttime.

   You want to know a secret?
   …My dreams are real.
    Every night.

        That boy'll grow to have problems.
           He'll be fine. Just a dreamer.

I dream about angels.
Teach her to stay.

       The professor says to find a theme
       And I call it unified irregularity,
       And I ask him if he dreams.

## Antipoeticism

There is a dark figure leaning against the wall.
He is an uninvited symbol
Humming, smoking cigarettes.
Someone else's creation,
The anti-poet.
He is a memory, he is a melody,
He is unavoidable.

*The blue smoke twirls around the solitary light,*
*All eyes are forced up, to the night...*

And when the sentence structure never mattered
Shall I compare it to a summer's day?
And when the words that failed me failed me,
They're just as pointless as the nouns.
The deconstruction of a soul.
What's the use questionmark
Shut your eyes symbolic dark.
The moment always screams depart
Screwing up the ends that start
Put the blindfold on your heart.
Put the blindfold on your heart?
I just don't give a damn.
Forgetting the aesthetics
Forgetting sciencing this art
Forgetting when it mattered
Forgetting, learning how.
There once was a flower
Boot mud run piss
There was a loved lover
Lie mate bruise kiss.
End rhyme is for morons with too much damn time.

Fine.
We've all reached for words,
As they floated like a metaphor
And when jaded lifes our situations
Clear as the mud on your face,
There is only saliva and thought.
The words are gone and helpless.

Tell the man to get off that wall,
They're all coming down.

## How to be Content

Well ladida your Derrida
(Don't pay attention I'm not real)
These words are empty, merely signs
Postmodern nonsense sometimes rhymes,
And soggy poems drip down drains
As things that change remain the same,
The structure of cold deconstruction
Is as complex as combustion,
And how fun it truly truly is
To explode the notions Hers and His.

It's just nihilistic discontent
Giving way to virtue bent
For what are morals but a box
With all emotions playing locks?

## After the Sunset

As the sun set, so too did our love.
Or yours anyway…

Now there are headphone notebook street corners at dusk
And candle-lit finger tapped keyboards on Friday nights.
In typical remembrance of your idealized memory
There exist corners for silent shaking
And beds I can sit on for days,
There are trees that will bend in silence
Displaying the undetermined route of aimless thought.
Now, presence and absence are one in the same
Carrying on in the honest moonlight of my solitary stroll.

A remarkably secret realization
Allows me to be everything.
I need nothing, because I can't have anything.
The grass is always greener in well-gardened yards,
And the sky is always bluer for louder hearts.
Yearning is a waste of time,
Like most worthwhile endeavors.

The scratching of my pen's seething mind
Stretching absently around delusion.
The soulless debris crashes against the cage of a man.
The barefoot rain awaits the dreams of an angel.

Objects are flying into walls, fists pound books,
And tears fall burning onto screaming pillows.
Yesterday's sadness is today's regret
Is tomorrow's confusion is—
There are galaxies hidden in the tears,
There are frantic stumbles in the night,

Circles of sadness moving physical impossibilities
To the depths of madness.
Moments are being noticed and captured
Moving so fast that the swirling is standing still
You can grab the colors
And wrap them around your thoughts—and pull.
The pain is unbearable, the pain understands.
It is only the night.
When the sun rises, I will sleep.

## Day One Again

It's so amazing this today here alone
The world just opened silently
And now is alive.
If I could call you right now I would.
If it wouldn't be too awkward
I would skip hello and say
You'll never believe the beauty
Of this mundane moment
And you really should come see
We will lock arms and silences
And laugh walkingly
Through this dream where we can
See the beauty, feel the moment
Skip hello
And hold to Spring.

## Scattered

Have you ever been so scattered,
So lost everywhere at once,
That now you're simply pieces,
Of a whole that's disappeared?

Are you ever sand, on boardwalk wood
The whim of any wind,
Joyless painless not quite not—
A truly helpless now?
When gripping tighter makes it slip
And home is where you land,
And there's so much sight at any time
That all you see is blur.
Have you ever been of so much sand
That a wind will run your day?
Lost and silent,
Scared and helpless,
Scattered.
Scattered gone.
Have you ever been of so much sand,
That you're everywhere at once?
And when you are, do you feel
That for the first time you are part?
The earth is you, and you're the earth,
Connected now at last.
Have you ever been so scattered,
That you can't help but feel alive?

## Spark of Something

You know that point right before you cry?
As your eyes water but before they break?
And there's that spark of something there
And it's barely even real but inexplicably too great.

And right at that moment there is no confusion,
But you still can't express it.
And the feeling's all consuming,
And there's no way you can repress it.

Well that is what you are to me—
That spark of something.
That pure emotion.
That all-consuming feeling in a powerful devotion.

So it doesn't matter if it's happy, or if it's sad
If it's rainbow colored, or just blue.
It doesn't matter what it is,
As long as it is you.

Because that is what you are to me—
That pure emotion so complete,
That spark of something bittersweet...
And as necessary as a heartbeat.

## Forget What I Said

Put your head back to bed and forget what I said
If I hurt anymore you'll be in love with the dead.

On a magic lit night, in the darkness of death
We cry at a wake
        For my wet weekend soul
Drinking down words
I say to keep you awake.
I'm obsessed with your eyes, crying
Tears like raindrops.
Raindrops like drinking on the weekends
Good music
        And candlelight.
I like, your eyes
Crying, I can barely see
A few hours in front of me
We will find ourselves lost
Where we usually are
Wishing for a star
To wish upon
To ride down from the sky
Crashing down into fires
Warming hours of cold
Made from years, now forgotten
We can't remember ourselves
Young and in pain
Mouthing out words
        To your eyes, crying.
If I hurt anymore, I won't make it through the night.

Put your head back to bed and forget what I said
        I am just a bad dream

Seeking salvation
In the light of your tired eyes—
Crying.

You are the moonlight;
I am the night.

## Wishes

I caught one of those floating in the air I tell you
And I let it go.
I didn't make a wish as they say.
You say you don't like wishes.
That's something you never used to say.
I guess there are a lot of things
We never said.
Maybe I should have wished
For less wishes.
Maybe we should have wished less.
You say wishes run out.
We never used to talk about ends.
I tell you it's just pennies
At the bottom of a fountain.
You don't gain or lose much, with wishes...

Mostly, I just wish to keep talking.
Our never ending conversation
Is one of the rare things, I still believe in.

## Shhh

I hope you don't mind
But I was telling the truth again.
Someone I hardly know, wrote me a letter
Reaching out I assumed
For anyone who could understand
The unexplainable tired torment
Or the maddening loss of control.
Her frantic letter had no commas.
It told the tail of cuts on her thighs,
The kind she couldn't explain
Even as the bloody blade
Was clenched under her white knuckles.
I'm sure you understand, the cuts
Were her rewards—
Placed gently on her safely hidden legs.

I wrote her back immediately
With commas, dashes, underlined phrases,
Adjectives and care.
I wrote about the cigarette
Put out on the left side of your chest,
And the fingernails that ripped in the underside
Of your tiny mighty wrists.
I described for her in detail
Myself, crashing against brick walls
Sleeping in the dirt
And muttering to you about wind chimes.
I explained the faces in the crowd
When I grabbed that microphone
Soaked from rain, making
The blood from my knuckles spread
As I read poetry about pounding

My fist against my heartache
And fighting back the tears.

I talked about the broken glass, on the concrete,
And how it cut me,
Because I could barely walk.
And I tell you, because I told her,
How I let someone hit me in the face.
How I let him, and I didn't fight back,
And I looked in the mirror, and I was proud
Of a bruise I didn't have to hide.
I was tired of lying.

I told her as much as I could
So that she would know it was okay
And that she wasn't alone.
I said that she was beautiful for it
And that I once fell in love
With you, not despite, but because
Of such a beauty.
I told her that you were not alone
And I wouldn't let you be,
And that it was okay.
Then I told her
That if you do it again,
Just one more time,
My next letter will not end so well.
My frailest control will shatter
Like the broken glass on which I once fell
And nothing will be hidden
And the final cut will not heal.
I told her to stay beautiful

But to be careful.
Her wounds could hurt someone else,
Even worse.

## Prayer

With my head on my heart and my heart in my words
I get lost in my sadness and the results are absurd.
I see Christ on the cross through the lies in my eyes
And I am thankful for all that may live laugh or cry.
With freewill in my being I may miss the real meaning
The truths are eternal,
                Only my mindset is fleeting:
I denounce my mistakes and then promptly repeat them.

By forgiveness I'm humbled, by existence I'm blessed
By the strength of his suffering I must better my best.
To remove my confusions and the lies which abuse them
I must ask for his blessings and the wisdom to use them.
With my head on my heart I'm my own worst pollution
Breathing the problem,
                As I search for solutions:
They are always right there if I'm willing to choose them.

When my heart won't stop hurting and my life is too hard,
I get lost in myself when I should be lost in my God.

## Things that Burn

Those concerned, with things that burn
Tend to disappear in smoke,
And lately it's so common
That I wake and start to choke.

I've been trying undying to believe in what you sell,
I've got lies wrapped up in hatred
I've got packages from hell.
I won't sell myself to sell my soul
I won't reverse it for a dime,
The lies by lies to gather lies
Is a waste of pointless time.
A Godless death-filled crime.

I've been living and giving cell not sell by cell myself,
I've got trinkets of my torment
I've got sorrow on a shelf.
I won't hate my dreams to make your days
I won't reverse it for a flame,
The pain on pain to harvest pain
Is a cruel remorseless game.
A hellish hurtful shame.

I've seen people in chairs
Boo the ones upon the stage,
And if you don't like what you're reading
I say burn this pointless page.

## Somewhere There Is a Voice

Somewhere there is a voice.
[I am talking about the human soul if that makes sense. The
word human is unnecessary backwardly descriptive as in
species form genus, packaging and propaganda (I see
graffiti marked trucks on autumn rain roads slow down
unrealistically focus on the wheel spitting violently rubber
on asphalt the color of clear between two layers of black and
you too would spit violently and jump from your wedge—
when it's wet don't squeeze too hard or the grip will slip)
                    Some                                    where
                                                            there

                    is: a voice.
They say you can't float without friction and we question if
you can really float at all, but we take the axiom as
presented afraid of images of faulty support beams (They
were weak with age. They blame wear on usage and we
wonder if you can really float at all).
Some                     where
                    there
                    here…
White noise is empty noise because it's without purpose, it's
dissident and I too have been dissident knowing that
sometimes white noise is a conglomerate of more
purposeful sounds—welcome to the confusion that builds to
end, piling on top of faulty axioms surrounded by wheels
autumn rain roads and clever packaging—I am talking
about the soul. I watch a wet leaf fall to the asphalt just slow
enough to render itself background noise.]
                    Can you here it?

# Split

There was a moment or a mirror
Something that cut my world in two
Split personified petrified
Hurled hurling in the wind
There was a mirror that showed me
I was not everything and everything
Could not rest in me.
I was very young,
And it was a very brief moment,
And I cannot remember.

What were once experiences of myself
Became other things.
The feeling of being touched
Was now a touch,
The sensation of cold
Was now the touch of an ice cube.
The images in the mirror were myself
And myself was something incomplete,
Something searching for the wholeness
It would never again believe in and
Never again know, as itself.
The moment,
Which previously would have been myself
Was now just a moment.

There are things afterwards,
Transitional things.
A red chair, white rock, bleeding pillow.
A frog the size of a small child,
A man with eyes the color of concrete,
Walls that cried in the summer,

And cars with evil intentions.
All of these transitional things
Become reduced to images
Just as myself is an image,
They are replaced by
Perception, condensation,
Inertia and sales tax.

The rest of eternity
Is bound in a photo album.
I flip through the pages
Searching for an image split like me,
To make me whole again.

This is necessary process impossible.
The moment was smoke and mirrors.
The mirror says hello
But means goodbye.
The time comes to search
For a symbiotic delusion.

The only comfort I can take
Is that the moment was just a moment
And whereas it could have been myself
Myself became a moment.
Equally brief, uncontrollable, and urgent.
There is no power structure.
There is no hierarchy,
No system of control.
Being this disjointed, may give me an edge
In the chaos.

## Setting Sun

I'm watching the sun set
On New York harbor
At the very moment of this writing.
A perfect red circle spreading
Two birds fly towards and
The sky and water glisten
And I write, and…
Let it never be said
I was too foolish
To know when
To put down my pen.

## Sneakers and a Sun Dress

Somewhere there is an imagistic correlative
For the loneliness from which I run.
She is wearing sneakers and a sun dress
Riding a bus through the city.
She stares out the window as if it doesn't exist,
She has no expectations.
Nobody celebrates new spring more joyously.

I can't sleep and I can't wake up,
I take my morning coffee with two sugars
At two in the afternoon.
I devour paradoxes without remorse.
I have no destination but tomorrow.
I fear nothing but myself.

She sits with a book under an oak tree
Flipping the cream pages
And never glancing at her little wristwatch.

Political pundits quietly play word games on my television,
And my stomach aches
From cheese sandwiches and orange juice.

Millions of years of evolution
Failed to give me the answer to my misery
As I bounce a tennis ball off the empty wall.

She finishes the book, lets her hair down, and smiles,
She loves a good mystery.
She likes when the protagonist wins
In a way he didn't plan.

I turn off the distraction
And stare blankly at the blank screen.
My mind aches with thoughts of universal factors
In a subjective culture.
How can I find transcendence today
As I run from myself into tomorrow?

As the dinnertime wind grows cool
A yawn forms on her pink lips
And she starts her walk to the bus.

I grow frustrated at the lack of epiphanies
The heat in my stuffy shut-window house
And my lonely museless musings.

I go for a cool evening-air walk
To clear my stuffy mind.
I stop to sit under an oak tree, and smile.

After hours of torturing myself
I am now relaxed in the mystery of life.
I may not understand it
But I know somewhere
These abstractions exist in actuality.

I know even loneliness can be transcended.
Maybe when I stop trying to figure out how.

## Piano Ballad

A comfortable chair and a piano ballad
Is the plan.
If I could shut myself off I wouldn't.

You call and I don't answer.
I call you back
And you say I should have known it was you.
Who else would it be?

I invite you over and you ask "for what?"
I have an extra chair.

The song plays seven times and you arrive.
For hours we converse rhythmically mad.
Your voice is like cotton
        Your laughter like glass.

The night is more than I never asked.

I only planned on my favorite piano ballad.
I should have known it was you.

## The Call is Coming From Inside

There are so many doomsayers
Giving in to all the lies.
The human condition is contingent on fear.
Every next moment can be as black as the last
And the answers can't be ugly
If we never stop to ask.
The sky is falling, the world is ending
The horsemen know your zip code.

The apocalypse is over fools.

The fear will seal the fate.
The negative energy will be negative reality,
Because it's evolution. It's darwinistic.
If you're afraid of lightning, stand still
And eventually it will find you.

Security is a pair of handcuffs.
Safety is a grave.
We will choke on a fear of choking.

## Small Talk

Have you ever listened
To the touch and feel small talk
Of any average people wasting time?

One is always trying to release their favorite stories
And the other always listens with a nod.
The stuttered rhythm pours in mindless words
And you know they're thinking
Something else behind eyes
Intently vacant, both warm and insincere,
And the only joy is to know that times goes on.

It's so sad the disconnection
That can bind our selfish worlds,
And how pointlessness can be a cold embrace.
It's so sad the way we wander
Through each other through the streets,
And how time can be like pocket change or rain.

Some nuisances are common parts of life.
We pass them on, and pass them through
Together disconnected wasting life.

# Sui

*…Hello?*
　　　　—Why do you create?
*Because I don't know how to do anything else.*
So you have no choice?
*I have a choice, but I wouldn't like it.*
Art or nothing?
*No. I mean, I could be a plumber,*
*But I don't know how to be a plumber…*


Voices into cell-phones carried away in the wind.
　　　　　　　　　　　Simplifying.
She is a brilliant artist, visually speaking.
I have been trying to speak visually for years.
　I'm the type of person who skips over detailed description
　　　　Paragraphs to quicker arrive at the dialogue.
　　It's a faster read, though sacrificing some symbolism.
　　　　　　　　　　　*…Are you okay?*
I'm a little nervous.


The world is split in parallel lies
Paralyzed by fear,
And polarized in deceit.
　　　　For every view, there is an opposing view.
They define each other
And are linked as the tracks of the freight train.
Innocence is a woman tied down
Screaming into her cell-phone,
*Reality is steel! Reality is steel!*


A good filmmaker would cut
Seconds before the violent impact.
A moment of dark and a jump to dialogue.

*But there's always a hero, always a savior.*
He's dead.
*He can't be dead, it's predestined.*
  *It's fate, Hollywood, and common sense.*
Heroes save the world by accident.
    They save their lover on purpose,
    And everything else is a byproduct.
*So?*
So his love was run over by a freight train,
And he killed himself.
*But what about a happy ending?*

Everywhere there is festering proof
Of God's progressive ascension
Further into madness.
    (Note: Ascension)

All people, are failed Gods.

I made a house of cards once.
God made everything else
Plus the house of cards.
We are all limited and diverted,
Lies are laid out linearly
As if anything could be as simple as cause and effect.

God knows the extremities of all things.

    Genius reaches the extremities and stops,
    And because genius is divine and
    All things divine are unlies and beyond
    Reality, it circles proving its own divinity

And begins to fade into madness.
This is the fully liberating plight of God.
God who chose not to be a plumber.

Suddenly there was a warm breeze, the kind of wind that
seems melancholy and wise, as if it carries a million
whispers from a dozen reincarnated worlds. The house of
cards came tumbling down hitting the glass table, almost to
demonstrate just how quiet the room was. I looked up
suspiciously at nothing in particular, wondering how such a
wind found its way in. I then looked down desperately at
the pile with the King of Hearts face up, looking back with a
knife through his brain.
He chose his brain, not his heart.

These days, heroes are suicidal.
*That seems violently counter-intuitive.*
Well they're all self-destructive in some way.
Otherwise they would be riddled with guilt.
*Why guilt? It's not their fault.*
Guilt is what separates them from the villains.
Without guilt they're homicidal
Or they wish to be martyrs, for a homicidal cause.
*How does guilt affect that?*
It connects them to the whole thing.
It helps circumnavigate the madness.
Heroes want love or nothing.
*And by nothing you mean death.*
What else would nothing be?

Circumnavigate is a pointless word.
No matter how useful

Some words are pointless.
Their function is clutter
And veiled homicide.
There is no male equivalent
For the word lesbian.
It is a backward tool of a patriarchal system.
Modern wars are fought for control
Of minds.
   Cause: Effective brainwashing
    Effect: Power.
A full heart can never be poisoned
But any mind can be lead, and poisoned.

An empty heart is a nuclear missile pointed at God.

He chose his brain, not his heart.
*He. He is a card. Just a card.*
He is himself, it doesn't matter what.
Are you, "just an artist"?
*No, but I'm also not, "just a piece of art."*
That's only because there's no such thing.

On the seventh day God rested.
That's the hardest part to believe.
I imagine God staring down, that whole day
Looking beyond the extremities, amazed,
At once curious and knowing
About what creations would follow.
Everything at once
   God and failed gods.
The extremities serving as a cage
Provided in benevolence.

*I'm nervous now too.*
                    About what?
*About my life. It seems so fragile.*
Life? Do you mean your breath
Or your worldly day to day structure?
*Structure.*
            It is a house of cards.
*Will it fall if I breathe too hard?*


Defect is difference, and difference is beauty.
The aesthetics of humanity
Are wrapped around our inherent failure.
There is no such thing as original sin (just beauty),
And conventional morality is a tool of liars.
Fate is a word designed to frighten,
To point your mind toward inconsistent actions
Unrelated to your nature.
We must trust the divine design
And embrace our own failure.
Defect is difference and difference is beauty.
There is a cap on our genius,
A benevolent cage,
And we have been provided with empathy and love
As tools of freedom.


I emerge slowly, shaky-kneed and rain-soaked, at sunrise.
The old house before me looms life-size and enormous, the
entirety of it closed off with yellow police tape. With slow
deliberate step, I feign courage as I bend under the barrier
and gravely approach the door—locked. Stepping off the
step, I move to my right and pull myself up to what used to

be a window (I have already broken it). I lower myself inside, surprised to find that I'm knee-deep in water. It is not rainwater. I can hear somewhere in the background a gushing sound. I turn to my left, where in another room I can already see the water changes shade. As I walk, the wood floor feels strange beneath me. Waterlogged and tired, as if it intends to remain in place only momentarily, as a favor to me. Once in the room, I can see the corpse submerged next to the table. The King of Hearts, still with the knife in his head. I lift the corpse shaking it and sobbing. The King of Hearts of all people… what sick irony is that? Certainly God is mad. I drop the corpse and see on the table that the king has left a simple note:

*Reality is steel.*

We have been forced to reconsider
Everything fundamental.
Knowing anything pre-established
Is a potential cause
We search for new methodologies
And become lost in the lies
Guiding freight trains.
In a state of constant confusion
Nothing is right or wrong.
Was anything ever hot or cold,
Or was it all just sensation?
Our heroes are sad and humble.
Sensationalism is saved for movie stars.

*Himself, Herself, Itself,*
        *Whatever it was.*
Maybe it was your self.

*Either way, it was too much for me.*
Too much to control?
*Too much to create.*
That must feel terrible.
                    *It hurts.*
Where does it hurt?
                    *I don't know.*


He chose his brain.


A young girl spends days in the library
Learning, unlearning, and searching.
She writes, "*Satan brought me flowers*"
On the desk where she sits
Lays her head down, and cries.
She doesn't know why.


Children are forced to grow up
Blindfolded
                Feeling
            Through the dark.
Picasso wipes his brush on a napkin
And the napkin sells.
God can't maintain a level of sanity
Long enough to wipe your nose.
Time is barbaric, a machete through shrubs,
The future devours itself
As the children grow up
Blindfolded. Feeling.
The fullest hearts, as they learn to grow,
Grow to learn,
That there is a mighty destructiveness

Within them.
The fullest hearts direct it in inward.

The world grows a little less real, than say,
The internet, or the works of Shakespeare.
"Natural Law," is the phrasing
Of a contemptuous language.
Nature is wild, and only people have laws.
The more we muddy these truths
With our disconnection and lies,
The less real it becomes.

A world of contradiction
Consumption and greed.
      Of power poverty and pain,
Cowards captors chaos,
Communications, power lines,
Parallel lies, liquid funds,
Paper cuts, e-books,
              Depots and despots.
Stuntmen, conmen, yesmen,
Starvation and limitless wars.
A world of festering proof,
Self-perpetuating and murderous.
      The ones with the fullest hearts
Know the self is perpetuating.
They point their destruction inward
So it can't murder us.

*If heroes are suicidal, then there are no heroes.*
I don't agree with that at all.
*It's true, it taints the goodness of it all.*

*Everything is ugliness and*
           *All I wanted was a happy ending.*
Maybe there is no end.
Maybe it never stops.
*And life is reduced to a game?*
Life is art. Chess is a game.


Oh it was several years ago now. For days he had been
sitting in silence, refusing to let anyone bother him. I felt
terrible for him. He was going through a lot at the time. One
bad thing after another. Finally one day he started speaking
to us again. I guess he had been reevaluating everything. He
wanted to talk about the possibility that God was mad and
getting worse all the time. We talked for a few hours and
then I had to go. When I came back he was passed out in his
own blood. A lot of blood. The glass table was smashed
under him, and there was a deck of cards scattered
everywhere. Thank God he was okay.


He chose his brain,
           Doesn't that speak something about heroism?
*I don't know does it?*
                    I don't know.
*Do you still carry that card with you?*
Yes. I carry a couple.
     For many years now.
*Why a couple?*
Just incase. Today for example,
                         I left one at the library.
I like to imagine that someone will find him
And maybe he'll help them somehow.
Help them as they try to think

About whatever it is that gets them.
*Gets them what?*
Gets them like us.
              *Alive like us.*
                            Right.


As God's creations
It's strange that we would search
For God in the heavens.
The full-hearted always seem to know
Where to start any search.
The empty-hearted however
Are normally preoccupied
And postoccupied
With pre and post apocalyptic
Thoughts of destruction.

              They aim their destruction outward
                 At everything hoping
                   To find themselves
                      Victorious
                                   In the wasteland.


*Does it make you sad, God being mad?*
No, why?
*Because maybe there's no help for us anywhere,*
*And worse, maybe God can't create anymore.*
*Maybe God is becoming futile and insignificant.*
I don't think so. It's an ascension into madness,
Not a descension.
God is becoming more godlike,
Becoming everything we fail to be.


70

Everything we would like to end up as.
*Except maybe there is no end.*
> Even better.

>> The in-between spaces are filled
>> With a silence which sings
>> Into a magical wind.

>>>> *…Hello?*
>>>> *Are you still there?*

Always.

>>> *Himself, Herself, Itself,*
>>> Myself.

## 2ⁿᵈ Half

It always seems.
And I'm so applause stop jump unbalanced—
As I watch you walk to,
But in the mist of grim subtle—
I don't think I'll ever forget how
And you sometimes came, mist
See by now we both know the
I keep wondering if hurt can—
And there is no.
And there is no.
I eventually, will,
Hiking on a tight-wire,
And then…
See you somewhere in the 2ⁿᵈ half of sentences.

## Not Saying

This is my not saying
Tired of make sense
Your blue is like a child
My childhood was willows
Let us secretly a yes
Departing sans all motion
The science of no points
Unlinear creation
On ice like how I was
With stardust on my if
Hidden for my clones
Created by conjecture
Lectured with a silence
From a gravestone singing snow
Warmer than a coffee
Brewing nothing full of life.
The opposites of knives
Bludgeoning a suntan
In surrealist anti-voice
To conceal historic noise
To reveal an avant-ploy.
I think genius is to silence
To dynamically shut up
I think I like this old not saying
I think that you make sense,
Like postmodern wet cement
With dents.
Beautifully bruised with flawlessness
Not saying.

## Because You Told Me To Pray

I found a strand of your hair
On the couch today.
I picked it up
And put it away, with the others.
Before sleep, I prayed to God
And thanked him for my treasure.
I asked him only,
That you would live forever.
I asked him simply
That when he takes me up to heaven
I be granted breaks, from time to time,
So that I may stare into your eyes,
And make sure you are safe,
As you sleep in his grace.

I told God the location
Of your letters and hairs
And how I keep them with the picture
Of you brightening the sun.
The one where you are smiling
Seeming happy with yourself
With my arm around your back
Around our moment nothing else.
And how I feel we've been that moment
Every minute since it was,
And how you looked the day I met you
And how I've lived under your love
And how the letters that you wrote me
Have torn edges and smudged ink.

And I told him of the flower
The one you picked me from the road

The day that we got lost, together,
Walking talking about life
And how I keep the petals safely
Just to prove that we were there.
I explained the way I felt, that day
To know you picked me from the road
And that everything you said of life
Meant I'd never be lost again.

And I even told God
About your favorite blue sweatshirt,
And how you wear it when you're cold,
And how cold can sometimes simply mean
Insecure, or scared, or tired.

I told God how I spent today with you
And about every word you said
And how blessed I am to have you
And how much that I would give.
I thanked him for this moment
And how it stretches without end
And I thanked him so relentlessly
And simply asked him if he knew
That all of these things
Have proven him true.

## He Asks To Carry Her Books

Haven't you ever seen a young boy
Carrying the books of a young girl?
I bet that's strange to you.
You miss the point.
The boy doesn't care
If the books are heavy.

I knew a poet who wrote
Mostly about sex and desire.
I always supposed the idea
Was to shock people with an honest
Portrayal of his own misunderstanding
Of his no longer secretive
Inner workings and thoughts.

When we're out and you're wiping
The dirt off my jacket,
It is because you don't want
My jacket to be dirty.

"Each sip of wine brings us closer to bed
Her legs cross. Uncross.
Her caress becomes haphazard. Impatient."
He would write.
I would say: red or white?
And he would say I miss the point.

I would tell him stories
About things you drew on a napkin
Laughter, rain
And how I didn't remember
What you wore (or

If I was tired).

It's true the napkin doesn't matter
Any more than the books
Or the wine. Or the jacket.
The point is
I am only impatient
When we're apart.

I would sooner carry boulders, with you
Than attempt to be without you.

## Seagulls

An older man, asked his friend
"What do you want to be
When you grow up?"
The second man, answered fast
"I want to be a seagull."

## It's Over

I wake sleepily in your bed
The cat at my feet
And see you have already left for work.

At your desk I put on my shoes
And write you an email:


Subject: It's over.

I'm sorry. It's not you it's me. While ignoring the problems
of our failed relationship I have developed a great
friendship with your cat. I have spent more time with him
than with you. Telling him our secrets.
I'm leaving you—and I'm taking the cat.


You call to ask if I'm serious.
About taking the cat?   Definitely.

Oh, about leaving you?   Probably.

You think I'm crazy
But I think I can't be with someone
Who doesn't even care about her cat.

## How Loud It Can Be

You'd never believe how loud it can be
In the middle of the ocean, in the middle of the night
The wind howls against the wavy black ink
And there are so many stars
It feels like you can grab them.
This is the nature of alone.

There's that feeling
When the wind is flying against your face
And if you turn your back to it
It is unpleasant and cruel
But if you stare windward and accepting
It is wonderful and liberating.

The world is dynamic and surprising
In the dark, you must feel your way through.
I have nothing left to prove to you
And I am just beginning to prove things, to myself.

## Wasting my Time

I'm a writer, who writes about writing
Wasting my time
And swallowing lightning,
Wandering lonely
While dying and growing
Assuming the symptoms
When there's no way of knowing.
Simply a child, who cries about sadness
Falling in love
And flirting with madness,
Trying ineptly
To never regret me—
Overflowing emotion
Can make you feel empty.

## Obsessive

I say I'm obsessive
And you say I'm addictive.
For a second,
I thought you meant addicting.

## I Know I'm Not Easy

I know, I'm not easy to love.
You know I know less each day,
I know you, you know what to expect.
We're making this more difficult.
If this is goodbye, well,
If it is,
Making it difficult will be the only way to lessen it.
But you know this already.

You often turn around, walk away, close your eyes.
This is to keep me chasing.
Or did you think I didn't notice?
If I refuse to follow you you will
Retreat still further, wear sunglasses
Turn off the phone and catch a train.
If I am silent you will hide, somewhere
So that no one sees you cry.
You will have to open your eyes
To let the tears out.
Look at me, I'm giving up.

Just because there is no one else
Doesn't mean I can't be alone.
If I stood in a snowstorm
Throwing stones at your window
Would it make you hate me?
If I built a fort like the kids do
Lined it with roses and
Left pages of emotion in a box
In the center,
Would you think less of me?
Does it make you angry

When I put my emotion in a box
In the center?
Would you prefer I carry you
Over the unshoveled streets?
It's cold out here, let me in.

You always make a point
Of keeping the attention on you
Your eyes searching the room
Planning their next move
Darting to the floor and
Fixing intensely at the moment of impact.
With you, it is always about points,
Scores, upper hands
Bells and whistles.

I always make the same point
Repeating myself constantly
As we walk to deny the gravity
Of our conversations.
You scrape your feet sulkingly
Dragging them as if to denounce their natural pace,
Your subtle form of control.
The product of your fear
Eternally afraid of letting go.

I've seen you smile honestly
I know it exists,
I know you're capable of ignoring the next moment
I know you can love without intent.
But I know I know less each day
I know you scrape your feet

84

And the concrete becomes my love.
My love should not be like stone.
I know, I'm difficult.

I care enough to stop chasing
To do whatever it takes.
You know what to expect
You know what I'll do.
Knowing this why do you carry on
Catching trains, scraping shoes
Keeping score
And leaving me out in the cold?
We're making this more difficult.
I know you know
I will lessen the impact of every goodbye.
I keep making the same point.
I want you to stop running
And let me in.
But you know this already.

## Apology

I have to apologize for the way I behaved
A child, confused and depraved.

With bottles of vodka on sleep deprived nights
My fingers refused not to type,
With my mind slipping desperate
To make something right
I grew recklessly lost in my plight.
I grew as near to far-gone
To completely insane
As has ever any ghost of its pain.
These excuses can't expect to explain.
Madness was life
And life was a game.
I'd be lying if I said that it's changed.

But now I can see that I only harm me
And I'm sorry that it ever was different
I never intended for you to be hurt
By the thoughts of my mad drunken fingers.
By the pain that had grown to indifference.
I never intended to get trapped in my symbols
Reality lost in my dreams
My words more important than their human effect
I was as mad as I maybe had seemed.
You were a Gatsby-like light shining green.
A symbol in a well-written scene.

I still haven't left the cruel world in my mind
But I've stopped dragging loved ones inside,
I will never forget the regret of goodbye

Or how real felt the tears that I cried.
I'm sorry to think what you must think of me
And I'm sorry if you have to at all—
In the face of the madness
And the realm of the mind
The universe seems timid and small.

I am saying I'm sorry for my young drunken heart
And my failure to handle the pain,
I am saying I'm sorry if I passed the pain on
I was just trying to keep myself sane.

## Spotlight on the Fool

Spotlight on the fool.
            Unheroic.
Motionless, building tension
               Dramatic.
If I stand here long enough, anything I say
Will go over big. Emphatic.
Anything said with certainty
Will be mostly believed, most of the time.
   The cameraman is shuffling
   Positioning pointing
      I can hear him click
I ignore him and pose,
                 Then I break.


A million dirty burn holes
From a million dirty lies
I can't stomach the lost love
From your black and dripping eyes.
There.
      The audience is hit, shot, shocked,
Stare intensely at the shadows
              Never stop talking
You are
      The open-casket poem-man
On display, in a cage,
In the spotlight,
        Bleeding on the stage.


It's funny honey now to think
The way we jump without a blink
To open arm's deceptive charms
To help the heart it always harms.

Never stop talking.

                You are in control
Lead them, ignore them
        Show them, honest
                                Open
Come, look,
            Slipping,
                        Raging,
Flooding.
            Watch.


As a child I filed away all my pain and I sucked it all down
and I wound up insane and I've grown up alone into a thing
you can't own although you've used me and bruised me
from the heart to the bone—I'm tired on fire and I'm sick of
the liars, the sneaks and the cheats and the way I feel weak,
the same old mistakes and the way that you're fake—I'm
sorry I'm trying but sometimes I break.
                        Stop.
Sudden,
        Dramatic. Emphatic.
                        The end.


There is nothing quite like, applause for your flaws,
The undeserved recognition, that will make your pain sick.

If I show you my weakness, maybe you'll tell me it's good.

## It Seems the Suicidal

It seems the suicidal
Are always preoccupied with isolation,
Of one sort or another.
It doesn't matter if they're the type
Obsessed with Sexton's "how"
Or if they're the kind that decide
Rashly and unexpectedly,
It doesn't matter,
They all live in mindworlds
At a bold, tirade set pace.
Your heart could write songs in Nirvana,
The rhythm could make Hemingway sing.

You never hear mourners in retrospect say
"His or her torture was all they had."
It's always some triumphantly beautiful
Absurdly talented
Unflinchingly unique
Shimmering life blinding light,
Flame that will never be replicated.
Even the ones that leave notes
Leave so much unfinished.
They never have the same priorities
They are not concerned with legacies,
Monuments or footprints.
They were never meant to be in this world.
Your soul could make anyone cry,
Their tears would be more precious than gold.

The suicidal ones, like you
Always seem a little more true to existence.
In a world where to know anything

You must create it yourself,
Where survival means mailing lists
And previously established concepts,
They are existing on the actual plane.
They are their own life force
Bursting all over the metaphysical truth
And warping any particles of matter
With their simplest imaginings,
With their solitary musings.
Your mind could baffle genius
Shelter millions
And reconfigure Earth's orbit.

You are the most astoundingly unique
Flash of brilliant uncontrived beauty
That this world never could have planned on.
That nothing could have foretold.

I suppose that is why,
You so honestly wish to die.

## Black and White

The black and white walls
Were a constant reminder of my insanity.
There was no gray, because gray is confusion.
If you want enlightenment,
Jump headfirst into madness.
Two black, two white—alternating.
A single force.

Wearing out the cassette, wearing sorrow and jeans.
The marble notebook margins were littered
With phrases of no importance.
Black ink promises
Polluted the white pages with the angst of a child.
Silent midnight paradoxes
Told myself to never give it up.
Always be the child,
At least the insanity was pure.

The force of the black ink promises
Against the ease of the pure white honesty.
A single force.
The black blinds tangled glimpses
Into the dark night yard.
The sunlight of schoolday gave way
To the quiet solitude of the room.
The blasting speakers could no longer be heard.
The cassette grew tired,
Screaming that no choice had to be made.
You can have your black, you can have your white.
You don't have to settle.
You're safe in this madness.
You were born for each other.

The only danger is forgetting…
The cassette said all this in silence.

I suppose I was always a confusing child,
And I suppose I always will be.
I sometimes perhaps use the word confusing
When I mean to say confused,
But that's a thought the kid
In the black and white room
Would disapprove of.
He would much rather believe
He gave me the answers, even then.
It was all so easy to figure out,
And I only sometimes worry
That he never stopped to ask if it was too easy.
Is it possible that he sent me
Flying into the impossible?
Is it wrong that he let insanity
Water the growth of confusion?
I know he would be angry to hear that.
I know he would press his black ink pen
Hard onto the page as he wrote
About promises and strength.
He would say to leave the confusion
To everybody else.
He would tell me I never have to explain myself
To the people of gray.
It didn't matter to him then,
Because he was both earth and sky,
Both seats and stage.

People ask me about the poems I write,

And I tell them that the poems write me.
I suppose the boy in the room wouldn't bother.
He didn't have to.
He had the room and the room was huge.
In all honesty, the room may have been limitless.
It was a simple thing,
But I still don't know
If it was simple in an incomplete way.
As I say that, I can almost hear him stabbing his pen
Against the book,
Creating a page of black specks.
The blackest of snows, everything crumbling down
And the boy delighted with the page,
Content to watch it all come down,
Like rain in the night.
He would love knowing that the people of gray
Couldn't understand that,
But he would never stop to dwell in it.
He had all the answers, and yet,
He is myself.

I have answers,
But do I have answers to questions?
Am I the disease or the cure?
Am I yesterday today or tomorrow?
Am I reality or am I fiction?
Am I alive or am I dead?
Am I the light or the dark?
Am I a poet, or am I a poem?
There's still all that gray,
And nobody understands,
When I say that I'm both.

The black and the white.

Today, the boy calmly types easy white words
Onto a silent black computer screen of promises.

## Upside-Down

Upside-down
I wrote this poem
When my world stopped making sense.

# Freedom

There's a dog on the rocks by the water
Peeing in the Harlem River
And my eyes are slits hung open
By eighty hour work weeks,
And a desire for a thing they call Freedom.

Freedom is a popular word thrown everywhere
Good for propaganda and sales.
It can mean God, home, money
Open roads, roadless lands, or fuel-efficient cars.

*What kind of dog is that?*
It is a brown dog.

Freedom is a day off or a lunch break,
Or the ability to staple your eyelids to your face
Or maybe to cut off a finger
Because you prefer the number nine.

A friend of mine once told me
That he's awake when he dreams,
And I thought that was a good way to be.
I sometimes think I'd like to sleep
In the middle of Times Square at rush hour.
It's just an idea I have.

*Do you think it's part German Shepherd?*
No. I told you, it's brown.
I've named it Freedom.
I think it belongs to a tree
About half a mile up river.
Now excuse me, I have to use the restroom.

## Finally, the Poet Speaks

My silence spoke volumes of your beauty.
"Speak poet speak."
I am, you're not listening, I am.

The wordsmith walks now on weary ankles
He left at your door.
The filthy masses on filthy streets
Rejoice in his heart,
Placed gratefully in your hands.
He walks slow and then fast
He spins smiles and remembers your face
A symbol of your soul,
The drumbeat of his wordlessness.
"Your eyes are like, your eyes," he thinks
That's a good way to explain it.
He drops ten dollars
      In a homeless man's cup
Turns the corner, climbs a tree
And sits for hours in the silent night.
Perched on top of the world, he listens.

The entire world, is speaking to you.

## Whispers in the Dark

Where are you?

*I'm here.*

No no, where are you?

*I'm right here. I will always be right here.*

Think about it. I want to know where you are.

*Well, where are you?*

I'm somewhere, 18 years old, without a trace of blackness around me. Instead it is all dark shades of blue, thick and light, like cotton in motion, with waves and tides. You are there minutely, in the form of only the tiniest spark of a notion. You are the singular star in my special surrounding skysea of blue. Between you and I floats somewhere a four seat table with two chairs on the same side, and it is made of smoke. It is perfect.

*...Is it a memory, or the future?*

It is a memory.

*Oh. So I suppose it was better then?*

No. It was painful as hell. But it's a perfect memory to dwell in. There I can know that someday I will find myself in a chair of smoke, with all the world's light in my hand, as around me it gets darker and darker.

*What are you saying?*

I want to know where you are.

*I'm somewhere, 18 years old, afraid that I'm losing my light.*

## And Sometimes a Friend

Phones, laptops
               And sometimes a friend
There is no need to stop
If the party won't end.
       Most people are terribly afraid of alone.
Some people
       Are terribly afraid of themselves.
                What else?

If I never let my pen stop moving
I will never have to realize what it is I'm trying to say.
If I never let my pen stop moving,
       I will never have to miss you.

I will never have to wonder about the world outside
Or where the noise actually comes from.
I mean the rumble, I feel it shaking
The foundation, of my never quite right.
If I never let my pen stop moving
I will never need my astounding memory.
I will never use my imagination to create
A comforting deathless magic.
I mean that harmless deathless magic playing dramatist
With a mystic therapist couch full of the inner goo.

If I never let my pen stop moving
I will never have to use my mind's capabilities
With all things layered
To pain myself to the edge of all understanding
Just to create one tiny ephemeral smirk
So I can almost feel momentarily okay
With how much I miss you…

Now that you're gone. You're gone.
This pen must help me to never know
You're gone.

I sit alone
(Now that you're gone, I'm alone a lot)
   Writing in this café
Watching everyone talking
To phones, laptops
            And sometimes a friend
And I imagine what they're saying is,
  "Never let me stop moving,
    Never leave me alone."

## Pink Setting Skies

Do you remember the memories lost?
Paying attention comes with treacherous cost.
There's no sense in the sensible options surrounding,
A staggering student of life and the sound in,
Everything everywhere pervasive alive,
People and passions and pink setting skies.
Mothers and fathers and children and trees,
The things that we are and the things we could be,
Brothers and sisters and parents and seas,
Me you him her ourselves them and we.

How many teardrops from some how many eyes,
How many smiles from some how many lies,
Too many sums from some some many parts,
Too many parts slowly tearing apart.

So many women and yes so many men,
So many families and yes so many friends,
So many us and oh so many them,
So many ends just to start new again.

Do you now know all the things you don't know?
Infinite learning as you live, as you grow.
There's no point in the pointless pretending and pondering,
Of minds lost in magic and mystical wandering,
Anyone anywhere exploding inside,
People and passions and pink setting skies.
Husbands and snowstorms and wives pets and stars,
We go in we go out we have walls floors and doors,
Houses and heroes and movies and cars,
Have need no yes mess less and more.

Here's to the past and the things that don't last
Here's to tomorrow, and to smiles and sorrow,
Here's to the heartache and the beautiful pain,
Here's to the sunshine, and yes, here's to the rain.

## Tumblesome Morning

I embark tumblesome into the morning
Prominently, if not creditably, insane.
Everything blurs as a hazy liquid grin
Lunacy in the moist humid city.

A pleasantly circular
Tropical flower of a woman
Sits to my right on the train.
The kind of flower that smells to stink
Obliviously perfumed to the point of sneeze
With pale skin in my way, from the corner
Of my sleepy sideways eyes.
I turn the pages of my madman novel
Thinking more people should smell
Like old literature.

I walk amusingly on worn broken shoes
Surprisingly light today perhaps
In response to the heavy air.
I delight myself with musings
Of lateness and responsibility
And how pointless the people seem
To stare pointlessly into this
Pointless cloud of a morning.
It's suddenly very important,
This wet and ridiculous anti-moment.
I try to think that one of these scared and
Not individual faces may be the face
Of someone plotting to kill me or
Lock me in a giant birdcage over
A greenhouse of tropical flowers.
I look each one in the eyes inquisitively

And delight in their examination
Of my shoes.

I dance mildly as I enter the office
Saying "morning Jack"
To Steve the manager, who quite typically
Informs me that I'm late.
I want to warn him about the birdcage
And accuse him of espionage
But instead I say "sorry Jack"
And tell him the weather
Really muffled my commute.
He says I'm full of excuses
And wishing I was, I grin
And do another dance asking
If he's seen my sorry shoes,
And we laugh pointlessly and insane.

The day begins,
And the wind blows another musty page.

## Labor Day Weekend

Exhausted from the long workday
I run out of the bar chasing
My cousin, because I know him.
Outside he steps in the middle
Of a commotion I would have ignored.
A man without shoes grabs a wood sign
As he charges a smaller man
Bloody-nosed and screaming
Lifting a garbage can in defense.
We grab the sign from the shoeless giant
And in what I can only assume is heroism
Stupidity drunkenness or instinct
My cousin slams the giant
Against a caged storefront,
Locking his head in his arms.
The scene is chaotic and ugly.
I wonder what Thomas Hobbes would say.
I never liked Hobbes.

The shoeless struggles and growls, to no avail.
My cousin tells him patiently to calm
As he pushes him to the wall.
His giant shoeless eyes are angry
Desperate and tortured.
I stand tense waiting
For it to get worse.
I try to convince the bloody nose
To walk home.

The thing Hobbes didn't understand
Is you can't expect to explain
The world from within

Parameters you've defined.
The world refuses to be this malleable
And really you can prove anything
With a structured analysis built solely
On presuppositions unproven and assumed.
I use a copy of The Leviathan
As my mousepad.
I bet he didn't count on that.

The police don't show up until later
At which point I'm already preoccupied
With the moon that always seems
To spend weekend nights on 7th
This time of year.
In my mind the moon might as well
Have been sipping scotch
Instigating the whole pointless night.
Absolutely indifferent as it watched
The savage shoeless giant in a headlock.

I suppose Hobbes wouldn't have noticed
The moon anymore than did the shoeless.
I suppose some things never change.
I've given up on trying to make sense of it.
We're all as unique as the moon,
And the world refuses to be bound.

## Daedalean Daddy

I tell you about my daedalean daddy
Five years gone,
And we laugh
      (Because we're used to this)
As we imagine his life.
I say I hope my little missing sister
Throws her tears at his face
And you tell me your father
Used to beat you,
But at least you knew he cared.
I say that I hate you, and you smack me
And we laugh.
      (Because we're used to this)

## The Walls

I tell you in this spacious room
As we lounge in its vast solitude
That I believe the walls have
Become the ceiling, the ceiling
The walls and (you can tell me
Anything and I would believe
Even that you were Queen of Atlantis
In a past life or a dream, somewhere)
You say you disagree with me and
In the room we feed on its silence
And I believe we have accomplished
Something remarkable under
This wall, inside these ceilings and
I believe you when you tell me
We are not alone, though you don't
Know why (and I can see you engulfed
In oceans of things, I can't understand
Swirling, loudly) but it makes sense.
Tomorrow you'll tell me nothing is right
And I will say that in itself is enough.
You will disagree with me and smile
Because you know you're a liar
And I will only believe what you believe.
The walls are the ceilings, Atlantis is gone
Nothing is right, and it's more than enough.

## Prayer

God the creator, the father, the light
Protect me from me, make everything right
Be loud when I'm evil
Help me see all my sins
Force me to stop my destruction
Before it begins.
I don't merit salvation, I don't warrant your grace
Help me live every moment
                    Like I'm not a mistake.
Through me show your presence
Through me present you,
Show the miraculous purpose
With which God makes a fool.

## Before I knew the Night Bus Schedule
## From Your House

I stand at the bus stop
For at least an hour
As it snows outside
The cemetery
And I tell an old man
Who must reside at
One of the gravestones
That I know I'm making
Mistakes with you
But that I'm young
And I don't care
And a wind blows
Dead leaves everywhere
And the man is gone
And I know he knows
This feeling
And is pleased with me
And the thought of you
Which keeps me warm.

## There Can Be No Pinhole

We are not so different, you and I
Growing up together
Wildly unapologetic.

When did you become so fragile,
So alluring and frightening?
I see my reflection in your wet eyes
And I am angry.

We walk in circles tonight
I think because we have been lost too often
Given up on destinations and apologies.

It's not that I'm not listening
But you are so small, so transparent
And the streets are too awake to be this empty.

You ask questions as if we're alone
Somehow not seeing my lie stretching over us
Perfectly shading everything completely.

There can be no pinhole.

Everything multiplies, in your eyes
It is simple and transparent.
You don't understand incompleteness.

The night stretches another five minutes
So that you can end where you began
And I can tell your hands of my getting home safe.

I will walk angry and reckless knowing

We are not so different, but for the lie,
And your hands, fragile and unshaded.

You drop something insignificant
And I pick it up, and brush it off.
Maybe it's my life.

                  The stars applaud.

It is a seamless performance.

## For Emily, and Those Like Her

When you flood the grass
It grows back thick.
When you wound the skin
The scars are strong.
But the easiest target
Is the one already hurt
And don't think they'll ever stop
Until you're buried in their dirt…

So many people of beauty and brilliance
Are trapped under oppressive clouds of negativity
Haunting hope and taunting dreams.
It is hard to hope in a world
Where the dark days pass by
Our dismal existence far too slowly
To appease our dreary minds.
The innocent, the kind
Those with open hearts and open eyes,
These special few shoulder the brunt.
These rare and precious few are engulfed
By a world draped in sameness.
Like sugar melting into tea, they disappear
Leaving their mark as an invisible sweetness
Unexplained by the dark surroundings.

The only way out is through,
So do nothing that doesn't celebrate
Your existence.
You can't expose someone who never hides.
You can't defeat someone who isn't competing.
You can't find fault where there is only truth.

114

To be yourself is simply to be,
To avoid any and every not.
To live within the wild affirmation Yes,
Always the incorrigible child of a moment
A little more fantastic than a dream
An emotion beyond words
The singsong embrace of a rainbow
Never a cog, but always a ripple.

All this understand simply:
The flap of a butterfly's wings,
A teardrop hanging on an eyelid's curve,
The clutch of five infant fingers,
The gust of a wind—
And the sound of alive.

They will not stop
And it will not get better.
Only you will get better.
Too strong to fail and too scarred to be hurt
You will be a magic spark in the darkness
A sweetness in the air
And a triumph of truth.
Eternity will bow in recognition,
And you will be yourself unmitigated.
And it will be beautiful
And it will be brilliant
And it will be you.

## First Past Last

This is the first poem after
The very last I'd ever write,
Because I know I said goodbye
But I want to say goodnight.

I hope you know I'll always love you
I hope you know I wasn't mad
And I will sing forever endless
If the silence makes you sad,
Because forever I can capture
It was defined for me by you,
And I'm just a foolish human
I never know what I should do.
Goodbye was just a costume
But goodnight is always true.

My compulsive typing
Mindless rhyming
Keeps on talking out of breath
And it lines up with the rest.
It's just lost depression
Under pressure
Simple symbol scars,
And blood can measure
Stormy weather
But not the circumference of the stars.
A circle is always endless,
But a line can stretch too far.

The truth is like a circle
And my words are like a line
Because the truth is never ending

But my words are ticks of time.
There are things you just can't measure
And some things you just can't say
And the truth is something breathless
That will sweep the words away.
I mean, now is now and A is A.

Now this is the first poem
That I've written since the last,
Because the last one is the first one
And the future is the past.
But my words are in these broken lines,
Simple segments, done and measured,
And they'll never wrap themselves around
A love that is forever.

So please don't doubt my true intentions
And pay no attention to my lines
The truth is just self-evident
And I could never say goodbye.

I'm just writing to wish you,
A good night.
Sleep well.